Contents

The Hand

John Townsend

Published in association with
The Basic Skills Agency

Hodder Murray
A MEMBER OF THE HODDER HEADLINE GROUP

Orders: please contact Bookpoint Ltd, 130 Milton Park, Abingdon, Oxon OX14 4SB. Telephone: (44) 01235 827720. Fax: (44) 01235 400454. Lines are open 9.00–6.00, Monday to Saturday, with a 24-hour message answering service. Visit our website at www.hoddereducation.co.uk

First published in 2005 by
Hodder Murray, a member of the Hodder Headline Group
338 Euston Road
London NW1 3BH

Impression number   10 9 8 7 6 5 4 3 2 1
Year   2010 2009 2008 2007 2006 2005

Illustrations: Pulsar Studio/Beehive Illustration.
Cover illustration: Janos Jantner/Beehive Illustration.
Typeset by Transet Limited, Coventry, England.
Printed in Great Britain by Athenaeum Press Ltd, Gateshead, Tyne & Wear.

A catalogue record for this title is available from the British Library

ISBN-10 0 340 90054 7
ISBN-13 9 780340 900543

1

Ghostly Stories

The house isn't there now.
But that hasn't stopped the stories.
Stories of strange things.
Stories of ghostly shapes
moving through the trees.
Of cold shadows in the graveyard.

The house wasn't far from the church.
Yew trees clawed the sky
around its tall dark chimneys.
But now it's all gone.
It was all cleared away years ago.
Now there are new houses
and small neat lawns.
No one would know about the past.
Not unless they watched.
And waited.

The church has hardly changed at all.
Not for hundreds of years.
It's just as it was when the stories began.

Kim knew about the stories.
She'd seen them in a book on ghosts.
It showed old pictures of the house.

It looked scary, she thought.
But the stories were all a bit far-fetched.
That was why she agreed to take a look.
To go to the village.
To show it was all nonsense.

She'd have a look around the church.
It could make a good article
for the college magazine.
She could take a few photos.
They'd show just a normal church
and that the stories were made up.

It was a hot August afternoon
when Kim set off across the fields.
The sun beat down
on the stubble and dry earth.
Small birds darted in and out of the hedges,
pecking at ripe berries.
Blue sky stretched above miles
of golden fields.

Kim left the track and walked
along the disused railway line.
It was cooler here in the shade.

She paused to take a swig
from her water bottle.
It went back in her bag
beside the notepad and camera.
This was the life, she thought.
She felt like a real reporter.
In search of the truth.

After a couple of miles, Kim climbed a stile
and headed through the woods.
She came out on to a lane
with a signpost pointing up a hill.
From the top of the hill she could see
for miles across open fields.
She saw some houses to her right.
It was then she saw the church tower ahead.
It stood against a bank of dark cloud.
She stopped to drink from her bottle.
A breeze stirred the trees. Like a sigh.

Kim had written up the story
of Henry Bull in her notepad.
In 1863 Henry Bull built a big house
for his wife and 14 children.
He was the vicar of Gorley.

He didn't know his smart new red-brick house
was built where a convent had stood.
Where a body lay buried in the earth.

The old story told of a nun who had died
in the cellar of the convent.
She'd been bricked up inside.
All because she'd been in love with a monk.
She was about to run away with him.
But they were caught.

He was hanged, as it was a big sin.
She was bricked up alive under the convent.
Ever since, people said they had seen
strange things.
Shapes in the moonlight.
Moving shadows across the grass.
A nun sobbing in the trees.
A man in a cloak searching in the fog.
A woman's hand clawing at the church door.
A hand with a gold ring set with a large ruby.
Like a shiny drop of blood.
There was something else about the hand.
Something very strange.
It had an extra finger.

2

The Woman in Blue

Kim walked up the path through the graveyard.
It was all very still and quiet.
She peered into the porch of the church.
It was cooler here.
Perhaps there would be something inside
to tell her about the old house
or the vicar from long ago.
There might even be something about the story
of the nun and the monk.

She turned the big heavy door handle
with a clunk.
It was locked. Solid. The door wouldn't move.
She'd just have to look around
the outside instead.
She reached into her bag for her camera.

It was as Kim let go of the handle
that she saw the woman.
Her dark shape was framed in bright sunlight
that spilled into the porch.

Kim gave a gasp.
'I hope I didn't scare you,' the woman said.
'Just a bit,' Kim answered
with a nervous giggle.
'I was trying to see inside the church.'
'I know, dear. I've been watching you.'

There was a rattle of metal as the woman
pulled a chain of large iron keys
from her cape.
'Watching me?' Kim looked startled again.
'Oh yes, dear. I'm always watching.'
She pointed up to the corner of the porch.
A CCTV camera pointed down at her.
'We have to keep a lookout here, you know.
After all, you can't be too careful these days,
can you?'

Kim couldn't see the woman's eyes.
The light was behind her
so her face was in darkness.
A blue hood covered her hair.
She seemed to read Kim's mind.
'It looks like rain,' she said.
'I always dress for the worst.
We could be in for a storm.
Do you want me to let you inside?'

'Yes, please. If it isn't any trouble.'
'No trouble. I've come to do the flowers.
They don't do themselves.'

She brushed past Kim
and rattled a key in the lock.
The heavy door creaked open
and she led the way into the church.
The smell of flowers
seeped out through the door.
It felt damp and cool inside.
Kim shivered as she looked around.
She read the plaques on the walls.
There was no mention of Henry Bull
or the nun. Nothing.

The woman was already busy
putting flowers into a vase.
Kim took the camera from her bag.
'Do you mind if I take a few pictures?'
she asked.
'Do what you must, dear.'
The camera flashed.
Once pointing at the altar.
Then again at the stained-glass window.
Kim put the camera back in her bag
near the woman's feet.

A curtain hung across the entrance
to the tower.
Kim pulled it back to see what was inside.
It smelled musty.
There was a sudden noise behind her.
Like a groan – but more than that.
A distant scream. A man's scream.
Turning round, she looked back to where
the woman had been doing the flowers.
There was no one there.
Nor were there any flowers.
The space was empty.
Kim was alone in the church.

3

A New Discovery

A chill ran through Kim's body.
The church seemed to become darker
and colder all of a sudden.
She felt scared.
The wind howled in the porch.
A steady clunking of the clock
echoed from the tower.
She felt very alone.

There was a pile of old books near the door.
A scrap of newspaper poked from one of them.
Kim bent down and took it out.
It was from a local paper.
The headline read:
'GORLEY – THE MOST HAUNTED VILLAGE'.
It was from a few weeks ago.
She began to read the story.

The paper told of people who once lived
in the old house by the church.
Some of them left
soon after they had moved in.
They heard and saw strange things.
Worrying things.
In the 1900s people heard whispers
in the rooms at night.
They spoke of footsteps on the stairs.
Two maids saw a nun appear in the garden.
People began to talk.

Then there was the story of a woman
who lived there 70 years ago.
She lived in the house in the 1930s.
One night something hit her face.
She was thrown out of bed.
Her name appeared in shaky writing
on the walls.
Then a message.
It warned that the house would burn down.
People came from far and wide
to stare at the house.
It was called the most haunted house
in the land.

13

In 1939 it all came to an end.
One night the house caught fire.
By morning it was just a ruin.
And that was how it stayed for years.
Till the bulldozers came.

Then the builders moved in.
New houses were built on the land.
Kim had seen houses from the lane.
She looked at the photo of the old house
in the news cutting.
She'd seen the photo before.
She'd read the stories, too.
They were well-known.
But the next part was new.
The latest part of the story
happened only a few weeks ago.

The owner of one of the new houses
was having a new garage built.
The builders dug down and found bricks.
It turned out to be an old cellar.
Its doorway had been bricked up.
Inside they found a skeleton.

A photo in the paper showed
a local 'ghost-hunter' pointing at the skull.
But that wasn't all.
Experts had done tests.
They found the skeleton was of a woman
who lived hundreds of years ago.
The bones of her right hand were unusual.
Her hand was most odd. It had an extra finger.
On one of those bony fingers was a ring –
with a ruby.
Stamped in the gold was a sign.
A sign of an old order of nuns.

Kim put the news cutting
back inside the book.
It was all a bit odd.
Could there be any truth in the stories
after all?
She just wanted to go.
To be back outside in the warm sunshine.
She reached out to turn the door handle.
It wouldn't move. It was rigid.
She was locked inside.

4

Trapped!

Kim shook the door.
She thumped against the solid oak.
It wouldn't budge. She began to panic.

What was going on?
First there was the strange woman
who'd vanished.
Now the door had locked on its own.
And now she felt an icy shiver.
It was freezing by the door.
How would she get out?
She felt trapped …
like the poor nun bricked up in her cellar.

17

The wind howled outside.
She heard a crack of thunder
echo around the church.
The door rattled as an icy blast
ripped under it.
She pulled and tugged at the handle.
It still wouldn't move.

'Help! Please let me out!'
She beat on the solid oak.
She kicked at the heavy wood.
The smell of flowers stuck in her throat.
But there were no flowers to be seen.
All that was there was Kim's bag.

She ran to fetch it.
She didn't really know why.
Maybe she could find something inside it
to pick the lock.
Her hands fumbled inside.

Suddenly she froze in a wave of fear.
Her hand had touched the water bottle.
It was frozen.
The water inside had turned to ice.

By now she was screaming.
She just had to get out.
She hammered on the door as she cried.
'Please. Help me!'
Her heart was pounding.
Her face was drenched in cold sweat.

She coughed as the smell choked her again.
But it wasn't the strong smell
of flowers this time.
It was something else.
Stronger. More deadly.
It was smoke.
Choking. Sticking in her throat.
The loud crackle of flames
filled the darkness behind her.
'Help! Let me out!'

Suddenly there was another sound behind her.
The rattle of curtain rings.
Kim looked back over her shoulder.
The curtain was moving.
Very slowly.
It was being pulled back …
by a single white hand …

5

A Fuss Over Nothing

Kim threw her head back and screamed.
Her fingers clawed at the door.
She kicked at it as hard as she could.
The tears rolled down her cheeks.
It was then that the latch lifted slowly.
The door moved and swung open
in a warm blast of air.
Bright sunshine lit her wet face.

A man stood in the doorway.
'Whatever's the matter with you,
young lady?'
She threw herself at him.
'You've got to help me.
There's a fire ... the woman ... a hand ...'

The man's face changed. He looked cross.
'Utter nonsense,' he said. 'Snap out of it.
There's nothing – look. It's all in the mind.
You're all the same.
You young girls just like to make a fuss.
A fuss over nothing.'

The man was in a long black gown.
He led Kim back into the church.

'Look. Nothing.
Not worth all that screaming, was it?
Some girls love to scream.
They like to get all worked up.
They read all that ghost nonsense
and believe it.
I tell you, it's all made up.
People should know better.
I've been the verger here for years
and I've never seen a ghost.
It's utter rubbish.'

'Verger?' Kim said.
She was stunned. Almost in a trance.

'I look after the place,' he went on.
'I saw you arrive just now.
The camera caught you.
I came to check what you were up to.'

Kim pointed to where she had seen the woman.
'Then you must have seen the woman
who let me in. In a blue hood.
She unlocked the door for me.'

'Don't be daft, dear. I keep it unlocked.
That's why I put the camera there.
To spy on visitors. I saw you go in alone.
There was no one else. Just you.
I can show you the video if you like.'

They went back out into the porch.
Kim blinked at the bright sunlight.
'Lovely day,' he said.
'But what about the storm?
I heard thunder and wind.'
'All in the mind.
You wanted to believe in it all, so you did.
Like the rest of them.
If I were you, I'd go for a long walk
in the sun.
Get rid of those daft ideas.
Clear your head of silly stories.
You young people like to make a fuss.
That's all it is. Just to get attention.
Well it won't work. Off you go.
You can put a few coins in the box
on your way out.'

Kim walked away from the church in a daze.
She felt the sun on her back.
A warm breeze dried her face.
She was still shaking. She felt such a fool.
Maybe the man was right.
Maybe she'd made it all up.
Was it all in her mind after all?
Perhaps people see strange things
because they want to.
But she hadn't wanted to!
She'd come to show this was just
a normal place.
Now she didn't know what to think.

Her head was in a spin
as she climbed the stile.
She sat in the shade
on the disused railway line.
All I need now is for a ghost train
to run me down, she thought.
But she couldn't smile.
It was time for a drink.
She opened her bag and looked inside.
She wasn't ready
for what she was about to find.

6

The Camera Never Lies

The camera was at the bottom of Kim's bag.
She took it out to take a closer look.
She'd taken two photos inside the church.
One showed the window.
It came up on the display.
Not bad.
The colours looked quite good, in fact.

She pressed the button
to show the other picture.
It flashed up on the viewer.
Very clear. Too clear.
It showed more than Kim had feared.
It showed a woman in a blue hood and gown.
She was holding a bunch of flowers
in her hand.
Her right hand.

Kim looked closely.
She clicked to enlarge the image.
The hand was very clear ...
with its gold ring on one of the fingers.
One of her five fingers.
A ruby shone like a drop of blood
right in the middle.

Kim sat back with a sigh.
What did it all mean?
She looked back at the image.
She saw something else
that chilled her blood.

Near to the woman was a dark shape.
She looked closely.
It was a man in a long robe.
He stood by the altar.
But the candles seemed to shine
right through him.

The man's arms were stretched
towards the woman.
Pleading. Begging.
In one hand he held a flame.
But he wasn't looking at her.
He was staring right at the camera.
A face with troubled eyes.
Desperate.
A rope hung from his neck.

Worst of all was his mouth.
It was open. Twisted.
As if he was choking.
Not so much coughing …
as trying to scream.
A scream that suddenly
burst through the hedge
and echoed around her.
It filled the tunnel of trees
and hung in the leaves above her,
before slowly drifting away
on the warm summer breeze.
To be drowned by the far-away call
of startled crows.